LIGHTNING BOLT BOOKS™

Endangered and Extinct Birds

Jennifer Boothroyd

Lerner Publications Company
Minneapolis

For Grace
—J.B.

Lerner Publications Company
A division of Lerner Publishing Group, Inc.
241 First Avenue North
Minneapolis, MN 55401 U.S.A.

Website address: www.lernerbooks.com

Library of Congress Cataloging-in-Publication Data

Boothroyd, Jennifer, 1972–
     Endangered and extinct birds / by Jennifer Boothroyd.
        pages   cm. — (Lightning bolt books. Animals in danger)
     Includes index.
     ISBN 978-1-4677-1330-6 (lib. bdg. : alk. paper)
     ISBN 978-1-4677-2493-7 (eBook)
     1. Rare birds—Juvenile literature. 2. Extinct birds—Juvenile literature. 3. Endangered
species—Juvenile literature. I. Title.
     QL676.7.B66 2014
     598.168—dc23   2013015572

Manufactured in the United States of America
1 — PC — 12/31/13

Table of Contents

Birds — page 4

Endangered Birds — page 6

Extinct Birds — page 16

Helping Endangered Birds — page 26

What You Can Do — page 28

A Remarkable Recovery — page 29

Glossary — page 30

Further Reading — page 31

Index — page 32

Birds

How can you tell this is a bird? It has feathers. It has a beak. It has wings. It has two legs.

This bird is watching the eggs in its nest.

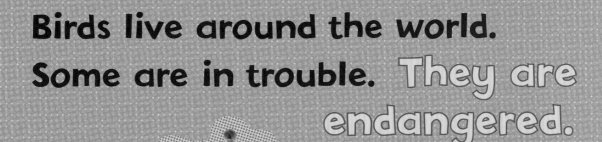

Birds live around the world. Some are in trouble. **They are endangered.** Endangered animals are in danger of dying out.

The Philippine eagle is endangered.

Endangered Birds

Look at those wings! The California condor is one of the largest birds in the United States. It is endangered.

> The wingspan of some condors is 9.5 feet (2.9 meters).

Condors are scavengers.
They eat dead animals.

The crested ibis lives in China.
These birds are endangered.
Their habitat has been
damaged.

A habitat
is where an
animal lives.

These birds use their long bills to find food in muddy wetlands.

They eat frogs and fish.

The Bali mynah has bright blue skin around its eyes. Its home is an island called Bali.

Bali mynahs are in danger of dying out.

The mynah makes many different calls. Calls are sounds birds make.

Too many of these birds were caught to sell as pets. Not many are left in the wild.

This tiny bird is the colorful puffleg. This type of hummingbird is endangered.

The colorful puffleg eats nectar from flowers.

The puffleg lives high in the Andes Mountains of Colombia. Pufflegs have fluffy feathers above their legs.

These are northern rockhopper penguins. Do you like their spiky feathers?

Not many northern rockhoppers are left in the wild.

These birds live on islands in the Indian and Atlantic Oceans. The penguins build nests on rocky ground.

Extinct Birds

Confuciusornis is extinct. *Extinct* is a word to describe an animal or a plant that has already died out. *Confuciusornis* was about the size of a pigeon. It used its wings to fly.

Confuciusornis lived more than 100 million years ago.

People learned about *Confuciusornis* by studying its fossils. Fossils are hardened remains of animals or plants.

The dodo was very unusual.
This bird had small wings.
But it couldn't fly.

Soft feathers covered the dodo's body. Its face did not have any feathers.

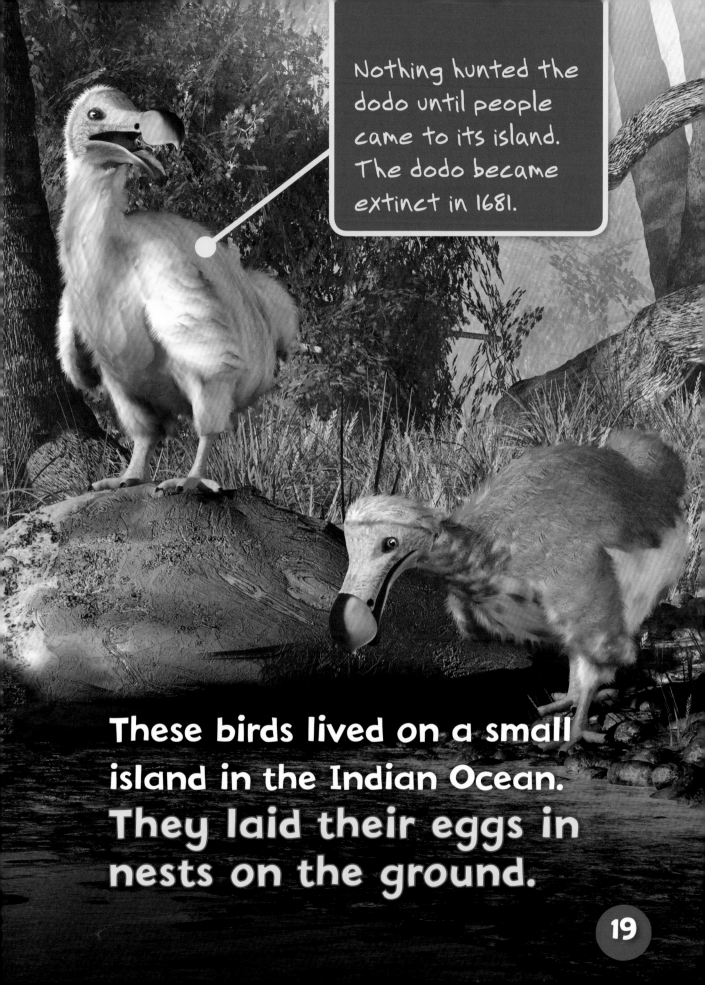

Nothing hunted the dodo until people came to its island. The dodo became extinct in 1681.

These birds lived on a small island in the Indian Ocean. They laid their eggs in nests on the ground.

Moas used to live in New Zealand. Some moas were huge. The giant moa could grow to 10 feet (3 m) tall!

The last moas died out less than seven hundred years ago.

female moa

male moa

common pigeon

Some laid eggs weighing
14 pounds (6 kilograms).
These birds did not fly.
They lived on land.

Moas ate seeds
and fruit.

Passenger pigeons were once found all around the United States. They had red feet and legs. The males had pink and bluish-gray feathers.

Passenger pigeons could fly very far and fast. They flew almost 60 miles (97 kilometers) an hour.

The last passenger pigeon died in 1914.

The Atitlán grebe became extinct after 1983. They were waterbirds.

This bird spent most of its time in the water.

These birds made nests on floating plants. The Atitlán grebe could swim underwater to catch small crabs. These birds could not fly far.

This lake is in Guatemala. The Atitlán grebe used to live here.

Helping Endangered Birds

A government official frees a bird caught by poachers.

Many endangered birds were hunted too much. They were caught by poachers. Poachers hunt animals illegally.

Responsible pet shops do not sell endangered birds. If you see one for sale, don't buy it! You can also help endangered birds by learning about them. Read about endangered birds in books or online.

You can research which birds make good pets. The cockatiel is one of many pet birds you can choose.

What You Can Do

There are many things you can do to help endangered birds.

- Clean up trash. Birds eat trash because they think it's food. Eating trash can make birds sick.

- Join a bird count. That's when people count all the different kinds of birds they see in a day. Scientists study these numbers. They try to find out whether any birds might be endangered.

- Don't use chemicals on your lawn or garden. Birds can get sick from eating chemicals.

- Support zoos and other groups that care about the health of birds.

A Remarkable Recovery

The bald eagle lives in North America. Bald eagles became endangered in 1978. Scientists had discovered DDT was making the birds sick. DDT was a chemical used on plants. Rain washed it into lakes and rivers. The eagles ate fish from the water. When they did, they also accidentally ate DDT. Then the government made it illegal to use DDT. Soon bald eagles were no longer endangered. By 2007, there were more than twenty thousand of the birds in North America!

Glossary

bird: an animal with wings, two legs, feathers, and a backbone

endangered: at risk of dying out

extinct: died out

habitat: where an animal lives

illegal: against laws or rules

poacher: a person who hunts illegally

scavenger: an animal that eats dead animals or dead plants

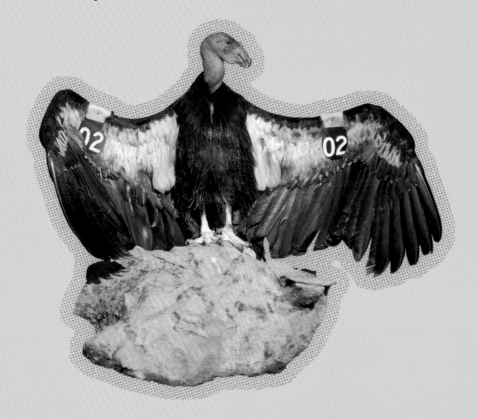

Further Reading

The Great Backyard Bird Count
http://www.birdsource.org/gbbc
/kids

Hoare, Ben, and Tom Jackson. *Endangered Animals.* New York: DK Publishing, 2010.

Laverdunt, Damien. *Small and Tall Tales of Extinct Animals.* Wellington, NZ: Gecko Press, 2012.

National Geographic: Last One Photo Gallery
http://ngm.nationalgeographic.com/2009/01
/endangered-species/sartore-photography

Neighborhood Explorers
http://www.fws.gov/neighborhoodexplorers

San Diego Zoo
http://kids.sandiegozoo.org/animals/birds

Silverman, Buffy. *Do You Know about Birds?*
Minneapolis: Lerner Publications Company, 2010.

Index

Atitlán grebe, 24–25

bald eagle, 29
Bali mynah, 10–11

California condor, 6–7
colorful puffleg, 12–13
Confuciusornis, 16–17
crested ibis, 8–9

dodo, 18–19

eggs, 19, 21
endangered birds, 5–15

extinct birds, 16–25

moas, 20–21

nests, 15, 19, 25
northern rockhopper
   penguins, 14–15

passenger pigeons,
   22–23
poachers, 26

Photo Acknowledgments

The images in this book are used with the permission of: © Angel/Wanless, pp. 2, 14;
© iStockphoto.com/w-ings, p. 4; © Edwin Verin/Dreamstime.com, p. 5;
© iStockphoto.com/PhotoPalle, p. 6; © Joel Sartore/National Geographic/Getty
Images, p. 7; Kyodo via AP Images, p. 8; © Xi Zhinong/Minden Pictures/Corbis, p. 9;
© Joanne Zh/Dreamstime.com, p. 10; © John Chellman/Animals Animals, p. 11; © Carl
Downing, p. 12; © Fundación ProAves/www.proaves.org, p. 13; Brian Gratwicke/
Wikimedia Commons, p. 15; © Bert Muller/Foto Natura/Minden Pictures/Corbis, p. 16;
© Layne Kennedy/CORBIS, p. 17; © Encyclopaedia Britannica/UIG/Getty Images, p. 18;
© Daniel Eskridge/Stocktrek Images/Getty Images, p. 19; © M. Bunce, T. Worthy/The
Oxford National History Museum, p. 20; © Roman Uchytel, p. 21; © Jack Thomas/
Alamy, p. 22; © Louis Agassi Fuertes/National Geographic Society/Corbis, p. 23;
© Philip Boyer/Science Source, p. 24; © iStockphoto.com/holgs, p. 25; FU JIANBIN/
Xinhua/Landov, p. 26; © iStockphoto.com/JLBarranco, p. 27; © iStockphoto.com/mrdaz,
p. 29; © James Deboer/Dreamstime.com, p. 30.

Front Cover: © Glenn Nagel/Dreamstime.com (left), © Dorling Kindersley/Getty Images
(right).